POWER MAGIC
Science Activities for Children

Alison Alexander and Susie Bower

Illustrated by Carolyn Scrace

SIMON & SCHUSTER BOOKS FOR YOUNG READERS
Published by Simon & Schuster
New York · London · Toronto · Sydney · Tokyo · Singapore

THIS BOOK BELONGS TO

POWER MAGIC

The aim of this book is to encourage children to explore ways of harnessing and using energy.

By making insects creep and dancers dance or through building a paper house, children can discover how forces and energy are used in machines.

Especially chosen to appeal to 6 to 10 year olds, the experiments are simple and safe. Using readily available equipment, they utilize the manipulative skills and abilities of this age group.

This book, with its easy-to-follow instructions, will stimulate children to adapt and develop their own variations of the experiments—an important point in the education of today's child.

Important note
Masking tape

We have recommended using masking tape as opposed to transparent tape. This is because it is easy to tear and stick, it can be painted over, and it is fairly water resistant.

SIMON & SCHUSTER BOOKS FOR YOUNG READERS
Simon & Schuster Building, Rockefeller Center
1230 Avenue of the Americas, New York, New York 10020
Text copyright © 1991 by Alison Alexander and Susie Bower
Illustrations copyright © 1991 by Carolyn Scrace
All rights reserved including the right of reproduction
in whole or in part in any form.
Originally published in Great Britain as
Power House by HarperCollins Publishers.
SIMON & SCHUSTER BOOKS FOR YOUNG READERS
is a trademark of Simon & Schuster.

10 9 8 7 6 5 4 3 2 1
(pbk) 10 9 8 7 6 5 4 3 2 1

Library of Congress Cataloging-in-Publication Data
Alexander, Alison, 1949—   Power magic :
science activities for children / written by Alison
Alexander & Susie Bower ; illustrated [by] Carolyn
Scrace.   p.   cm. — (Simon & Schuster books for
young readers)   Summary: Presents experiments for
exploring ways of harnessing and using energy.
1. Force and energy—Experiments—Juvenile literature.
2. Power (Mechanics)—Experiments—Juvenile literature.
3. Science—Experiments—Juvenile literature.
[1. Force and energy—Experiments.   2. Power (Mechanics)—
Experiments.   3. Science—Experiments.   4. Experiments.]
I. Bower, Susie.   II. Scrace, Carolyn, ill.   III. Title.   IV. Series.
QC73.4.A45   1991   531'.6'078—dc20   90-19930   AC
ISBN 0-671-74131-4   ISBN 0-671-74130-6 (pbk)

Manufactured in Hong Kong.

Contents

Make a Boat That Goes Like a Rocket

You will need:
small plastic or polystyrene tray like those
 used for packing food in supermarkets
2 flexible drinking straws
2 balloons
masking tape
Handi-Tak ® or other reusable
 plastic adhesive
sheet of paper
pencil
jam jar lid
scissors

Make two small holes in one end of the tray
large enough for the straws to fit through.

Fit the balloons onto the end of the straws
nearest the bendy part and seal with tape.
Test that the joint is airtight by blowing up
the balloons through the straws. This will
also stretch the balloons and make them
easier to blow up later.

Next, slide the straws through the holes so
that the balloons are resting in the tray.

To make funnels to hold the balloons steady in the boat, use the jam jar lid as a pattern and draw two circles on the sheet of paper. Cut them out as shown and tape them around the straws to form funnels. Then tape them to the side of the tray to keep them in place.

Blow up one balloon and seal the end of the straw with Handi-Tak ®. Then blow up the other balloon and seal that. Lower the boat into the water and remove the Handi-Tak ®. The boat will zoom away.

Why it works
As the air stored in the balloons rushes out through the straws, the boat is pushed forward in the opposite direction. In the same way jet engines and rockets are propelled forward by the escaping gases from their burning fuel.

5

Fly a Kite That Never Fails

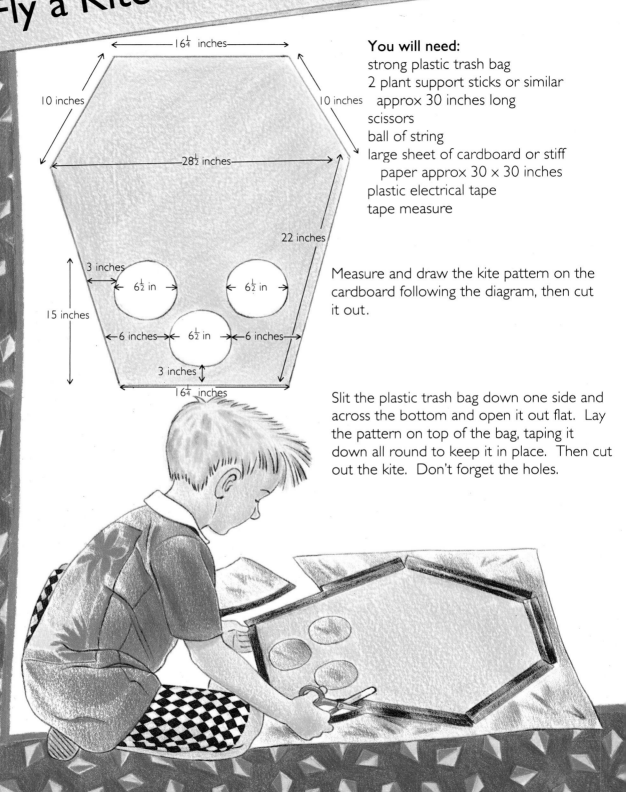

16¼ inches

10 inches   10 inches

28½ inches

22 inches

3 inches

6½ in   6½ in

15 inches

6 inches   6½ in   6 inches

3 inches

16¼ inches

You will need:
strong plastic trash bag
2 plant support sticks or similar
    approx 30 inches long
scissors
ball of string
large sheet of cardboard or stiff
    paper approx 30 x 30 inches
plastic electrical tape
tape measure

Measure and draw the kite pattern on the cardboard following the diagram, then cut it out.

Slit the plastic trash bag down one side and across the bottom and open it out flat. Lay the pattern on top of the bag, taping it down all round to keep it in place. Then cut out the kite. Don't forget the holes.

Using plastic electrical tape, fix the sticks in position, then make two small holes for the string by pinching up the bag and snipping it across. They will need to be reinforced. To do this, fold pieces of tape around the edges as shown. Tie a piece of string about 35 inches long between the two small holes then tie a knot in the middle to form a loop about 3 to 4 inches long. Now tie the loose end of your ball of string to the loop.

You can decorate the kite using paints or self-adhesive colored labels.

To fly the kite, face into the wind and hold the kite behind you (or get a friend to help). Start running, letting go of the kite and letting the string out as the wind catches it. Even if it is not very windy, the kite will stay up as long as you keep the string short and keep running.

35 in

Why it works
Although you cannot feel it, the air all around you pushes against anything it touches. The design of a kite affects the way the air moves and pushes around it. This kite is designed to fly at an angle so that there is more air flowing below it than above. This means there is a greater force pushing upward than downward, so the kite stays up.

Waterworks

Pinch the bottle to make the first cut.

You will need:
empty dishwashing liquid container
plastic straw
scissors
masking tape
pencil
corkscrew

Cut the top off the container and then cut panels out of each side as shown.

To make the funnel, remove the lid from the top of the container. Turn the top upside down and tape it securely to the sides of the container at an angle.

Careful!

Using the corkscrew, make two holes opposite each other in the side panels of the container. Smooth the ragged edges by pushing the pencil through the hole and twisting it around. This is so that the straw will turn freely when pushed through.

To make the wheel, use the panels from the container. Cut four pieces, approximately 1½ inches × 2½ inches. Fold them in half lengthwise, and tape them together to form a paddle wheel as shown. The size of the wheel will depend on the size of the container. It must be able to spin freely.

Push one end of the straw through one of the holes in the side of the container, then through the center of the wheel and through the hole on the other side. Tape the wheel so that it is firmly fixed to the straw and moves with it.

Pour water down the funnel and the wheel will turn. You could put string around a small yogurt container and attach it to the straw. See if the wheel will wind it up.

Why it works
The force of the falling water makes the wheel turn. This energy can then be harnessed to power any machinery or object attached to the wheel axle.

Take All Your Things Upstairs !

You will need:
2 empty thread spools
2 plant support sticks
ball of string
carrier bag
masking tape
Handi-Tak ® or other reusable
 plastic adhesive
glue
scissors
cardboard

Cut four circles of cardboard about 2 inches larger in diameter than the ends of the spools. Make a hole in the center of each one and glue them on.

Push a spool onto one of the sticks so that it rests in the middle. Then cut two pieces of string about 20 inches long and tie them on each side of the spool as shown. Fix the free ends of the string to the upper stair rail. This is the top pulley.

To make the bottom pulley, cut a piece of string four times the height of the top stair rail and tie one end of it near the middle of the second stick. Push the second spool onto the stick, fixing some Handi-Tak ® on the other side to keep it from slipping off, but allowing it to move freely.

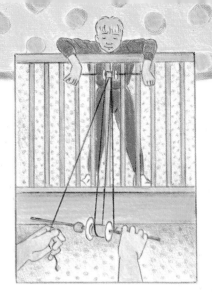

Get a friend to hold this stick just below the one already tied to the stair rail, then wind the long string over the top reel, down and round the bottom reel, over the top reel again, and finally down to the ground.
Go down and lower the pulley as your friend lets it go.

Put the ends of the stick through the handles of a carrier bag, put your things in it, and wind up the string. As you do, all your things will be lifted easily upstairs.

Why it works
Pulleys are machines that allow you to use less effort to move a heavy load. Although you use less effort than if you lifted your things directly, you will find that the length of string you pull will be three times the height that your things have traveled. The more pulleys you have on a system, the heavier the load you can lift.

Disco Dancers

Near one end of the box make two holes in each side, opposite each other, large enough for the wider straw to fit through and to turn freely.

You will need:
shoe box with a lid
scissors
masking tape
2 thin plastic straws
2 wider plastic straws
1 flexible straw
2 pins

To make cogs, cut the lid in two sections about a quarter of the way along. From the larger part cut four circles about 2 inches across and make the edges wavy. Make a hole in the middle of two of them large

enough for the wider straw to fit through. Push the straw through the hole in one side of the box, through the two cogs, and through the other side of the box.

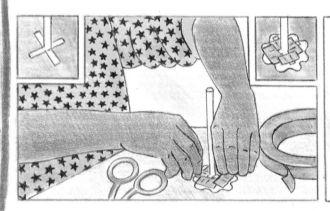

Take the two thin straws and make four slits in one end of each straw. Bend the sections back and tape them firmly to the middles of the other circles. Rest the lid on

the box. Near each edge, directly above the straw pole, make a hole large enough for the straws to turn freely.

Take one of the wider straws, cut it in half, make four slits in one end of each half, bend the sections back, and tape them over the holes in the lid. Push the cogs along the pole so that one is below each hole.

Lift the lid and push the two thin straws up through the wider straws. The cogs attached to them should rest on top of the lower ones, as shown. Push a pin through each thin straw just where it sticks out above the wider one. This will keep it in position. Tape the lower cogs firmly to their pole so that they turn with it. Finally, tape down the lid.

Cut out two dancing figures and tape them to the thin straws. To make a handle, fix a small section of the flexible straw over the end of the pole. As you turn it, the dancers will move around.

Why it works
When two objects move against each other, friction is always there trying to stop the movement. As you turn the handle, the cogs on the pole touch the dancers' cogs, making them turn. This is because the friction between the two cogs keeps them from slipping. This demonstrates how cogs are used in machinery to change the direction of movement.

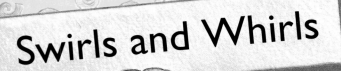

Swirls and Whirls

You will need:
wooden baseboard
assorted jam jar lids
nails $\frac{5}{8}$ to $\frac{3}{4}$ inches long
hammer
drawing paper
felt-tip pens
masking tape
self-adhesive mounting tape or squares
large cup hook
wide rubber bands or a spool of
  adhesive tape

Make circles of paper by drawing around each lid. Cut them out and find and mark the center of each circle (see diagram on page 5). Set them aside, remembering which circle fits which lid.

Cut squares of self-adhesive mounting material to fit the width of the lid. Stack three squares together and stick them to the edge of the lid. Repeat at roughly equal spaces around the lid. Then tape all around. Glue the circles to their lids and decorate them with patterns.

Place one of the larger lids near the edge of the baseboard and hammer a nail through the center point. Enlarge the hole slightly by moving the lid. Make another hole near the edge of the lid and push the cup hook into it to act as a handle. Turn it and the lid should whirl around.

Take the next lid and position it so that it is pushing against the first lid. Hammer it in place. Turn the handle and both lids should spin. If they are difficult to turn, enlarge the hole in the second lid slightly until you can get them turning freely together. Do the same with a third lid. See how many lids you can get moving at once.

If the lids begin to lose contact with each other, fix a rubber band or strip of adhesive tape around the edge to increase the friction.

Why it works
The adhesive pads on the lids form teeth that interlock, so that when the first lid is turned, it drives the second lid around, and so on. Each cog will turn the next one in the opposite direction, and smaller lids turn faster than larger ones.

15

Make a Paddle Boat

You will need:
smooth plastic soft drink bottle with a lid
2 sticks
masking tape or waterproof tape
plastic ice-cream container lid, or something
  similar (rectangular)
scissors
rubber band

Tape the sticks, one on each side of the bottle, about three-quarters of the way down. Make sure they stick out behind.

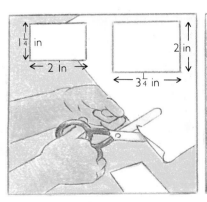

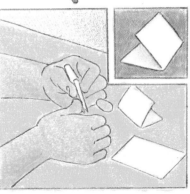

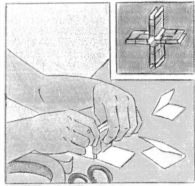

Cut four rectangles from the ice-cream container lid to make the paddle. The size will depend on the size of your bottle. For a 1 liter bottle you will need $2 \times 1\frac{1}{4}$ inch paddles. For a 2 liter bottle,

you will need approximately $3\frac{1}{4} \times 2$ inch paddles. Fold the rectangles in half lengthwise and tape them together all around to form the paddle.

Slip the rubber band over the ends of the sticks. It should fit comfortably between the sticks without being stretched too much. Position the wheel in the middle of the rubber band and wind it up counter-clockwise. Let the boat go in the bathtub and it will shoot forward. If you wind the paddle clockwise, the boat will go backward.

Why it works
The boat is driven by the energy stored in the twisted rubber band. In this case, as the rubber band unwinds the paddle turns, pushing the water backward and the boat forward.

Creepy Crawlies

Careful!

You will need:
empty thread spool
stub end of a candle about $\frac{1}{2}$ inch thick
2 matchsticks or cocktail sticks broken into
    approximately $\frac{1}{2}$ inch and 1 inch lengths
masking tape
sheet of paper
small saucer
scissors
crayons or paints
small safety pin
rubber band about 2 inches long
glue

Make the candle stub flat and even on both ends with the scissors. Using a corkscrew or the scissors, if they are pointed, carefully enlarge the hole down the middle. Pull out the wick and make a small groove across one end of the stub. This groove will hold the longer matchstick in position.

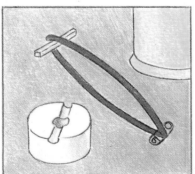 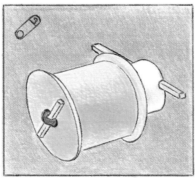 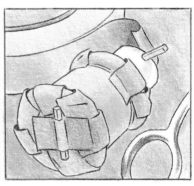

Loop one end of the rubber band over the shorter matchstick and hold it in place while you loop the other end through the safety pin. Thread the pin down through the spool and the candle stub. Put the end of the rubber band around the longer matchstick, resting it in the groove in the candle. Remove the safety pin.

Tape over the short stick to keep it in place and tape around the edges of the spool to give it a better grip as it moves around.

Draw around the saucer and make a paper cone in the same way that you made the funnels on page 5.

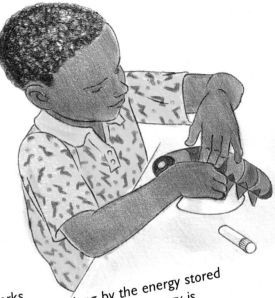

Cut out large paper insect shapes, color them, and glue them to the top of the cone, bending the legs down to disguise the cone.

hy it works
he insect is driven along by the energy stored
n the twisted elastic band. The energy is
released as the rubber band unwinds.

Wind up the spool by turning the matchstick round and round until you can feel that the rubber band is fairly tight. Put the spool down, quickly place your insect on top, and watch it crawl around!

Why it works
The insect is driven along by the energy stored in the twisted rubber band. The energy is released as the rubber band unwinds.

Build Yourself a Paper House

You will need:
a pile of newspapers of different sizes
masking tape

Tightly roll up a sheet of newspaper and tape the end down firmly. If you have trouble making the roll rigid enough, use three sheets together or roll them around a plant support stick and remove it afterward.

By using a variety of large and small newspapers or rolling them diagonally as well as straight, you can make different sizes of rolls.

When you have a large pile of rolls, tape them into triangles, squares, and rectangles. From these shapes you will be able to build a variety of structures – from domes to wigwams. The smaller the shapes are, the stronger the finished structure will be.

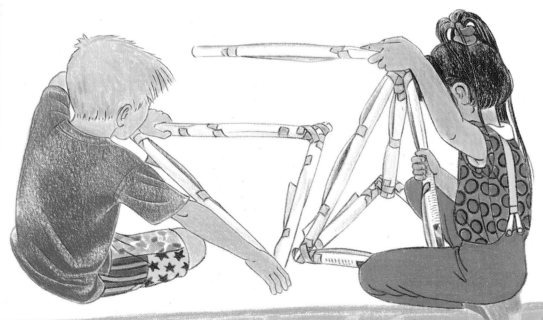

When you have finished your house, tape sheets of newspaper over the structure to make it private.

Why it works
These paper buildings do not collapse because the paper has been made stronger by rolling it.

A Suspension Bridge

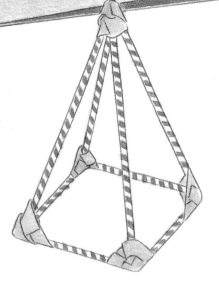

You will need:
package of straws
ball of thin string
masking tape
drawing pins
sheet of cardboard the length of the bridge
scissors
2 large rectangles of strong cardboard or
  wood to act as tower bases

Cut two straws in half and tape them into a square. Take four straws and tape one at each corner of the square, then tape the tops together to form a pyramid. This is the first tower.

Tape two towers side by side on each baseboard. Make three more towers in the same way.

Tape two straws about halfway down between each pair of towers to make a platform for the roadway.

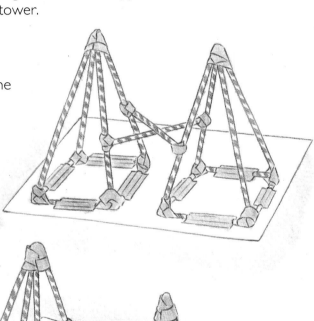

When you have decided how long the bridge is to be, cut two pieces of string that will stretch from one base, over the top of a tower, across to the other tower and down to the base on the opposite side. Fix these in place, tying them to the top of the towers and pinning them to the bases.

Cut the cardboard roadway and make holes down both sides about 1 inch apart. Rest the roadway between the platforms and weigh it down to keep it in place while you finish making the bridge. Weigh down the bases as well, if necessary.

Cut a piece of string twice as long as the bridge, tie one end to the string at the top of a tower then thread it down through the first hole in the roadway, up through the next hole, over the string rail, down through the next hole and so on. Finish by tying the other end to the string at the top of the tower on the other side. Do the same for the other side of the roadway.

Why it works
In this suspension bridge the towers do not collapse because they are built to be strong enough to withstand the tension, or stretching forces, in the string. Because the roadway is held up by the strings, you do not need supports in the middle of the bridge and larger widths can be spanned.

Remove the weights, make cardboard ramps up to the roadway, and your bridge is ready to use.

Ghostly Lights

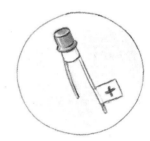

You will need:

sheet of cardboard
paints
4 LEDs (Light Emitting Diodes – these can be bought cheaply in electrical parts stores and come in red, yellow, and green)
plastic-coated wire for batteries
9 volt battery holder (made from a small matchbox, and 2 round-top paper fasteners)
9 volt battery
self-adhesive labels
wire cutters
scissors
masking tape

First make the battery holder:
Place the battery in the matchbox and mark where the two connecting points (terminals) touch the end. Take the battery out and at each of these points push one round-top fastener through the box.

Replace the battery so that the terminals touch the fasteners. You may need to wedge some paper at the other end to make sure the battery always touches the fastener tops. Slide the lid onto the box.

Each LED has a long wire and a short wire already attached to it. Make sure you write a + sign on the labels and stick them to the long wires as soon as you take the LEDs out of the package.

Now the picture:
Paint a picture on the cardboard, and when you have decided where you want the lights, make small holes and push the LEDs through so that the wires are behind.

Cut three lengths of battery wire so that you can connect all the lights up together.

Use the wire cutters to strip off $\frac{3}{8}$ inch of the plastic coating at each end of the wires.

Connect these lengths of wires to the LEDs by twisting them together. It is important to connect the long wire of one LED to the short wire of the next one. Tape each join to the cardboard.

Now measure and cut two pieces of wire to reach from the two end lights to the battery holder. Strip $\frac{3}{8}$ inch of plastic coating from each end of the wires and connect them up. The + terminal on the battery should connect with a + wire of an LED and the − terminal with a short wire.

You can make the lights flash by leaving one of the wires to the battery loose and just pressing it against the fastener when you want it to flash.

Attach your picture to a T-shirt and you can wear your lights!

Never connect just one or two LEDs to a 9 volt battery or you will damage them.

A 9 volt battery is not powerful enough to cause an electric shock, and it can't generate enough heat to cause a spark or fire. WARNING: Never experiment with the electrical outlets or wiring in your house.

Why it works
The power stored in a battery can only be released and harnessed when a complete circuit is made. This is done by connecting the lights with wires to the + and − terminals on the battery.

You can alter the battery holder to hold two 1.5 volt penlight (AA) batteries (enough to light up just one LED). For instructions, see page 26.

Burglar Alarm

3¼ in

3¼ in

You will need:
2 1.5 volt penlight (AA) batteries in a
   holder
3 volt buzzer or bell (available from
   electrical parts stores)
plastic-coated wire for batteries
thick corrugated cardboard
aluminum foil
2 round-top paper fasteners
scissors
wire cutters
masking tape

Adapt the holder on page 24 by fixing a
strip of aluminum foil across the end
opposite from the fasteners. Place the
batteries side by side, with the positive ends
in opposite directions. Make sure they are
always touching the fastener tops and the
foil.

Cut two squares of cardboard about
3¼ inches × 3¼ inches and make a hole
through the center of each square. Then
cut two pieces of wire long enough to reach
from under a mat outside your door to the
place where you are going to keep the
buzzer inside your room.

Using the wire cutters, strip off $\frac{3}{8}$ inch of the
plastic coating at each end of the wires.

Push the end of one wire through one of the
holes in the cardboard and bend it flat
against the other side. Position a 1 inch
square of aluminum foil over it and tape all
round it. Do the same with the other square
of cardboard and the other length of wire.

Cut four ridges out of corrugated
cardboard and stick the wired squares
together, using the ridges to keep the foil
pieces from touching until they are pressed
together. This part of the alarm goes under
the mat outside the room.

Using a length of wire that has $\frac{3}{8}$ inch of the
plastic coating at each end stripped off, join
the battery holder and the buzzer together.

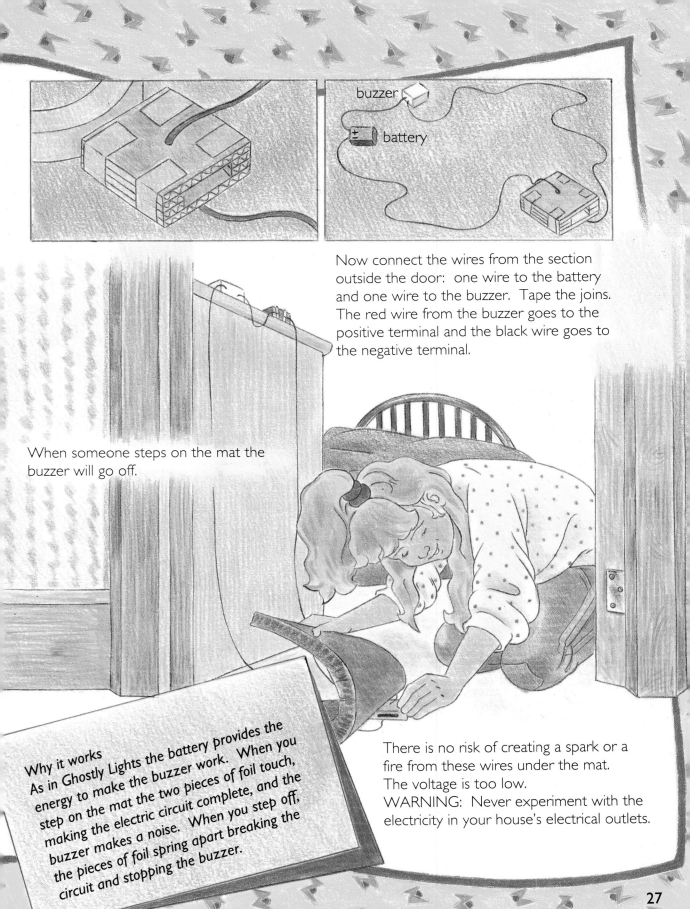

buzzer

battery

Now connect the wires from the section outside the door: one wire to the battery and one wire to the buzzer. Tape the joins. The red wire from the buzzer goes to the positive terminal and the black wire goes to the negative terminal.

When someone steps on the mat the buzzer will go off.

Why it works
As in Ghostly Lights the battery provides the energy to make the buzzer work. When you step on the mat the two pieces of foil touch, making the electric circuit complete, and the buzzer makes a noise. When you step off, the pieces of foil spring apart breaking the circuit and stopping the buzzer.

There is no risk of creating a spark or a fire from these wires under the mat. The voltage is too low.
WARNING: Never experiment with the electricity in your house's electrical outlets.

Make a Compass to Guide You

You will need:
small margarine tub or similar round
  container with a watertight lid
waterproof marker pen
large needle (e.g. darning needle)
spare tub lid
magnet
empty thread spool
plastic straw
masking tape or waterproof tape
scissors
waterproof glue
egg cup or small jar top

Glue the empty spool to the bottom of the margarine tub. While the glue is setting, use the egg cup or a small lid to draw a circle on the spare tub lid. Cut out the circle. Make four slits in one end of the straw, bend the sections back, then tape these to the underside of the plastic circle.

Cut the other end of the straw so that the circle will stand about $\frac{3}{4}$ inch above the spool when it is slotted in the hole.

Careful!

To magnetize the needle, stroke it 20 times with the magnet, using a circular motion. Always start at the same end and always be careful to lift the magnet off the needle after each stroke. Afterward make sure you put the magnet far away from the needle.

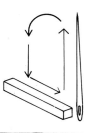

Tape the needle to the plastic circle and slot the straw into the spool. Fill the tub with water so that the plastic circle just floats and moves around freely.

The needle will point north/south. Use the position of the sun in the sky to help you decide which is which.

If you have a watertight lid you will be able to use your compass to guide you on walks.

Why it works
When you stroke the needle with a magnet, the needle becomes magnetic also. All magnets point to the north pole when allowed to swing freely because the strong magnetic force of the earth always pulls them in this direction. As long as the needle is not dropped or knocked, it will remain magnetized.

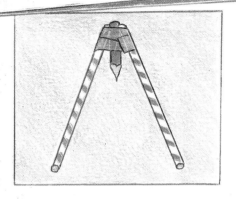

You will need:
short pencil about 2 inches long
2 straws about 4 inches long
scissors
Handi-Tak ® or other reusable
  plastic adhesive
drawing paper
felt-tip pens
masking tape
pen or pencil with a wide flat top

Firmly tape the two straws to the pencil so that they hang down at an angle and are rigid.

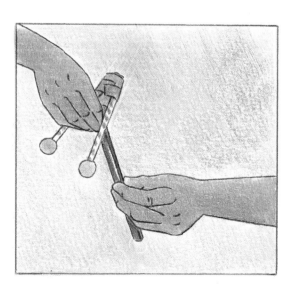

Wrap a small piece of Handi-Tak ® around the bottom of the pencil just above the point and stick two fairly large equal lumps onto the end of each straw.

Test whether the whole thing balances upright on a flat-topped pen. If it does not, adjust the balance by adding or taking away Handi-Tak ® from the ends of the straws.

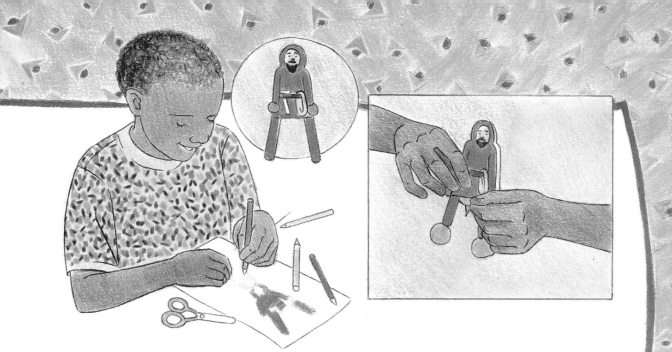

Fold the drawing paper in half and draw a mountaineer to fit over the pencil and straws. Color it in on both sides, and cut it out, leaving it joined at the head.

Fold the mountaineer over the pencil, pressing him into the Handi-Tak ® at the base to keep him in position.

Balance him on the pen top and see how far you can tip it before he falls off. If you stick the pen into a lump of Handi-Tak ® on the table, you can also spin him around. You can experiment with pencils and straws of different sizes.

Why it works

The earth exerts a force on everything, pulling objects toward itself. This force is called gravity. The center of gravity of an object is the point at which this gravitational force appears to act. The mountaineer will not fall because the two weights he is carrying put most of his weight below the pencil top on which he is balancing. It is important to consider the center of gravity of any object you design, to make sure that it is stable.

Make the Octopus Go into the Cave

Bend the straw round as far as it will go and cut the ends off so that you are left with a length of about 2 inches.

Cut the octopus out from the margarine tub lid. Its body should be about 1 inch long and its legs 1 inch long too. Attach it to the straw, using the paper clips. One half of each clip should go up inside the straw. Draw in the eyes with the pen and then test that the octopus floats upright by putting it in the bowl of water. If it does not, add another clip or fix a small piece of plastic clay or adhesive near the base of the body until it does.

You will need:
2 liter plastic soft drink bottle with a lid
flexible straw
paper clips
margarine tub lid
plastic modeling clay or reusable plastic
   adhesive
waterproof pen
scissors
black paper
large bowl of water

Cut a rocky shape from the black paper and tape it round the bottom of the bottle. Fill the bottle with water and put in the octopus. Make sure the bottle is full to overflowing then screw the lid on tightly.

Why it works
When you squeeze the bottle, water is forced into the straw, making the octopus heavier so that it sinks. When you release the pressure on the bottle the water comes out of the straw, making the octopus lighter again so that it floats to the top.

Squeeze the bottle hard and the octopus will dive down into the cave. Let go and the octopus will float up to the top of the bottle